MUSCLE-UP THE GUT OF YOUR STORY:

HOW TO WRITE THE NOVEL

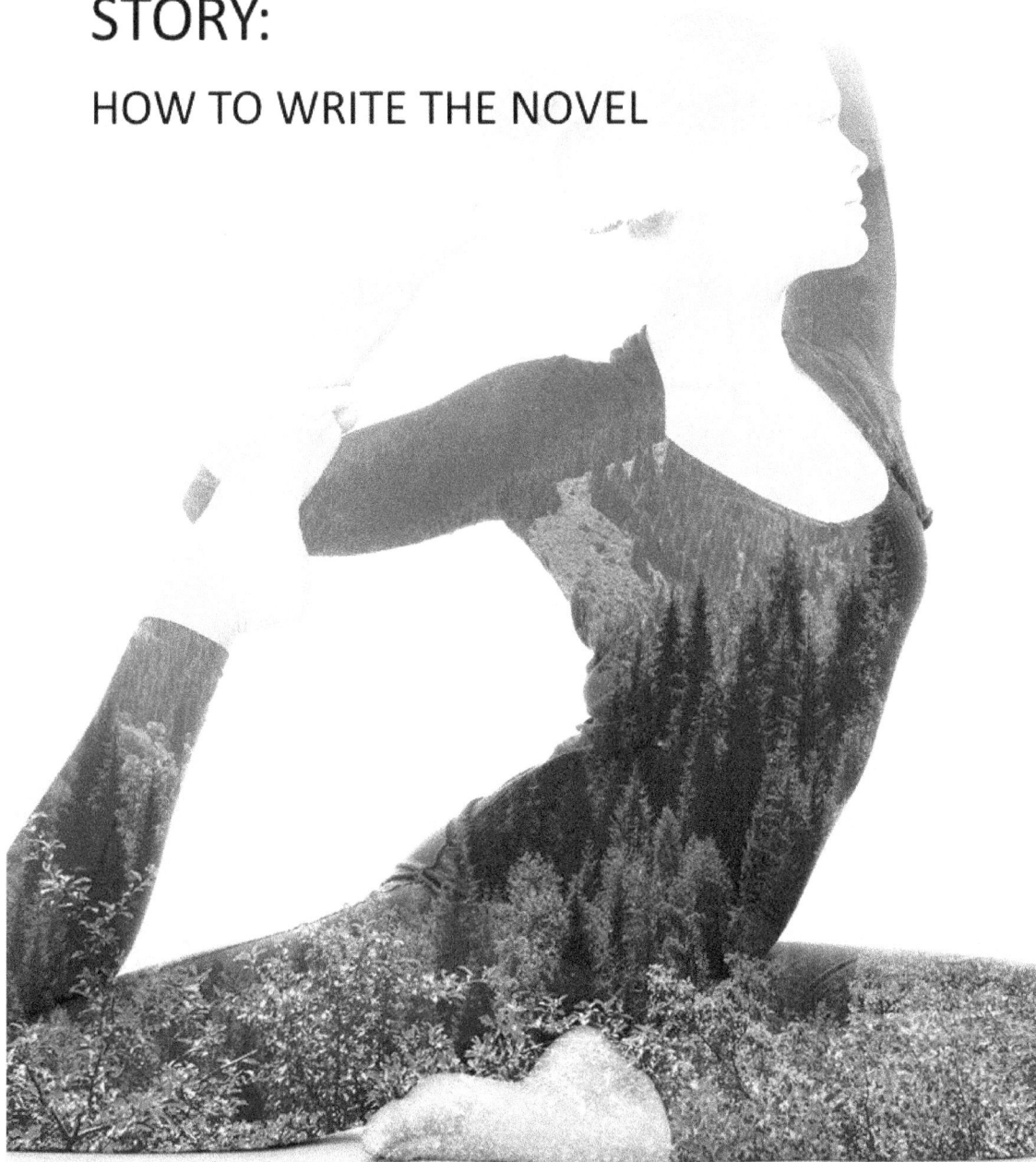

SUSAN WINGATE

SELECT TITLES ALSO BY SUSAN WINGATE

<u>NOVELS</u>
The Last Maharajan
Way of the Wild Wood
The Deer Effect
Troubled in Paradise: A Love Story
Bobby's Diner
Hotter Than Helen
Sacrifice at Sea
Of the Law

<u>SHORT STORIES & POETRY</u>
Catitudes & Platitudes
More Ravings
Ravings of a Mad Gentlewoman

<u>NONFICTION</u>
Tell Don't Show: How to Successfully Break the Rules of Fiction

MUSCLE-UP THE GUT OF YOUR STORY: How to
Write the Novel

Susan Wingate

Roberts Press
An imprint of False Bay Books
www.robertspress.com
Seattle, Washington 98126

USA

First published by Roberts Press, 2016

Muscle-up the Gut of Your Story: How to Write the Novel has been taught as an in-person workshop and taught online via Skype and other electronic means

Wingate, Susan.
[Nonfiction, How-to Write]
Muscle-up the Gut of Your Story: How to Write the Novel: nonfiction / Susan Wingate
pages   cm
ISBN 978-0-9898078-4-5 (paperback)
1. Title

Printed in the United States of America

Designed by Awesome Book Designs

TABLE OF CONTENTS

About the Author   9

Introduction   11

A Great First Page   12

Elements of Plot Development   14

Elements of Story Structure   15

Suspense & Tension   16

5 Distinct Parts of a Critical Moment   25

Sample Novel Outline   27

In the Beginning   29

The Middle   37

The End   39

POV Narrator   41

On Character "Voice"   43

Psst! Let Me Tell You the Secret to Voice in Writing   46

Your Character Chart   48

Writing "The End" and Now the Real Work Begins   58

Blank Pages for Notes   59

A Big Thank You   75

Bibliography   77

ABOUT THE AUTHOR

If you want to read award-winning, fiction steeped in suspense and sometimes set in mythical lands, or books with mystery and thriller elements, you will enjoy reading **SUSAN WINGATE'S** books. The twists and turns of her stories and her likable, touching characters are always unique. People say that her work is reminiscent to the fantasy series, The Chronicles of Narnia written by C.S. Lewis and also to the superhero Spider-Man series–books with unforgettable heroes and fantastical worlds readers can escape to. Susan Wingate's bestselling, award-winning books are recommended for teenagers, young adults, and for the young at heart! Susan began writing as a child when she learned her father was a writer. Susan Wingate writes fiction and is currently working on a gritty faith-based apocalyptic thriller series. Susan offers writing instruction to emerging writers at writing conferences, libraries, and online webinars. Her popular workshop "Muscle-up the Gut of Your Story: How to Write the Novel" has given emerging novelists the impetus to complete their first drafts quickly and efficiently. Susan also teaches writing craft, nuances about the publishing business, and how to market your book. Her workshops have been endorsed by many writers who have been struggling in their careers and have then gone on to get major publishing contracts with legacy publishers.

Becoming an Author

Susan has been writing from a very early age. She began writing as a child when she learned her father was a writer.

If you're a Kindle user, you can find all of Susan Wingate's books at her Amazon Author Page.

"My mission is to write evocative, compelling fiction for the reading public and to glorify God in the process. Anything less means failure." ~Susan Wingate

What Susan Says About Herself

I like to play golf. I want to learn to fly planes. I've parasailed in Mexico, in Ixtapa-Zihuatanejo, to be precise. I ride horses and love animals of all kinds. I'm learning to sing. I'm one of these people who removes spiders from the house and then sets them free outside. I save moths from spider webs when they get caught. This frustrates the spiders who I have saved but what do you do? This is what I call a "conundrum."

I live on five acres of rural land that is heavily wooded and is home to a herd of deer who I feed. I feed all the wildlife here, the raccoon and birds alike. We have eight cats, three dogs, and nine birds–ring neck doves and pigeons who are mostly rehab birds.

I enjoy eating chips and salsa to the point of addiction. I don't think there are any rehab centers for chip-and-salsa-addiction but maybe if we all ban together we can show the powers-that-be how devastating this addiction is to one's hind-end. I'm sure we'll see growth (wink) in that area of "intervention-need" soon.

Pizza is second on the list of my food addictions. So far, Papa John's has a fortress-strength special interest group blocking the way for any rehab facilities for pizza addiction. It's a conspiracy, I tell ya.

Hmm. What else? I am a homebody. And, why not? What, with all the animals, land, pizza, and chips and salsa around here, why should I leave my couch? I write on the couch. Some of my greatest moments have happened right here on this couch.

Anyway, that's me in a nutshell. Nut being the operative part of the word. Oh. And I write books–a lot of them. And I sincerely hope you enjoy reading my stories.

INTRODUCTION

I started teaching *Muscle-up the Gut of Your Story: How to the Novel* in 2005 when the local community college invited me to teach there when I inquired if they were looking for someone to teach a novel writing class.

I had recently finished my first and second novel when I began instructing this workshop. Since then, the class has changed a bit but not that much. I've updated it and fine-tuned parts but overall the workshop is the same as it was in the beginning.

The idea for this workshop began when I noticed a lack of such classes available in person or online. Since 2006, there has been an explosion of online classes offered as webinars. *Muscle-up* has been taught via Skype, at libraries, for private groups and at regional writing conferences. *Muscle-up* has given emerging novelists the impetus to complete their first drafts quickly and efficiently. Susan also teaches: writing craft, nuances about the publishing business and, how to market your book. Her workshops have been endorsed by writers who have been struggling in their careers but who have gone on to get major publishing contracts with legacy publishers.

How to Use this Workbook

Please note that this workbook discusses thrillers and mysteries as its overall example of novel-writing but understand that structuring the novel using Susan Wingate's method can be used on any of the fiction genres, from literary fiction to commercial fiction.

A GREAT FIRST PAGE
BEGINS BY CONNECTING THE READER WITH YOUR PROTAGONIST

The following items list ways to create a great first page, or what the publishing industry calls "a hook." A hook is an ever-compelling leader for the reader to continue reading to the next page.

Here are some ideas for a great first page:

Is one where Something is happening on that first page and does NOT include a character musing about something from the past or a bird flitting in a tree or just thinking about, whatever.

On this first page, what happens is dramatized in an immediate scene with action and description plus, if it works, dialogue—action and description can also be applied to literary and mainstream novels. Such as Karen E. Bender's A TOWN OF EMPTY ROOMS where she begins her story this way:

- She did not intend to steal anything that day. Serena Hirsch was walking through midtown Manhattan on her lunch break; it was one week since her father had died, and it was her first day back at work.
- In this example—you get the character hook dramatized and action, setting and information about her state of mind. All compelling arguments for excellent first page writing.

  What happens moves the story forward? The above example is also perfect in that, I don't care if you're a man or a woman, you will want to know more about the character—what Serena Hirsch has stolen and why!

  What happens has consequences for the protagonist. Again, what happens after Serena Hirsch steals?
- The protagonist desires something. This can be the item Serena Hirsch has stolen or something more deeply-seated like the wish that she can turn back time.
  - The protagonist does something. Serena Hirsch can lie which will
- Propel the story deeper into plotting and outcome.

  There's enough of a setting to orient the reader as to where things are happening. We're told in the above example that she is walking in midtown Manhattan. Period. We can flesh out detail later when they are absolutely necessary and not a moment before.
- Your first page happens in the NOW of the story. We do not start with:
- Backstory... What backstory? We're in the NOW of the story, nor do we include:
- Set-up... What set-up? We're in the NOW of the story.

  What happens raises a story question—such as: What happens next? Or, why did that happen? Why did she do it?
- A First-page Checklist—Protagonist
- It begins connecting the reader with the protagonist

- Something is happening. On a first page, this does NOT include a character musing about whatever.
- What happens is dramatized in an immediate scene with action and description plus, if it works, dialogue.
- What happens moves the story forward.
- What happens has consequences for the protagonist.
- The protagonist desires something.
- The protagonist does something.
- There's enough of a setting to orient the reader as to where things are happening.
- It happens in the NOW of the story.
- Backstory? What backstory? We're in the NOW of the story.
- Set-up? What set-up? We're in the NOW of the story.
- What happens raises a story question—what happens next? Or why did that happen?

Caveat: a strong first-person voice with the right content can raise powerful story questions and create page turns without doing all of the above. A recent submission worked wonderfully well and didn't deal with five of the things in the checklist.

FOR MORE WRITING HELP, GO TO: www.susanwingate.com/writingresources

ELEMENTS OF PLOT DEVELOPMENT

If an author writes, "The king died and then the queen died," there is no plot for a story. But by writing, "The king died and then the queen died of grief," the writer has provided a plot line for a story.

A plot is a causal sequence of events, the "why" for the things that happen in the story. The plot draws the reader into the character's lives and helps the reader understand the choices that the characters make.

A plot's structure is the way in which the story elements are arranged. Writers vary structure depending on the needs of the story. For example, in a mystery, the author will withhold plot exposition until later in the story. In William Faulkner's "A Rose for Emily" it is only at the end of the story that we learn what Miss Emily has been up to all those years while locked away in her Southern mansion.

So, What Goes into a Plot?

- Narrative tradition calls for developing stories with particular pieces--plot elements--in place.
- Exposition is the information needed to understand a story.
- Complication is the catalyst that begins the major conflict.
- Climax is the turning point in the story that occurs when characters try to resolve the complication.
- Resolution is the set of events that bring the story to a close.
- It's not always a straight line from the beginning to the end of a short story. In Ernest Hemingway's story "The Short Happy Life of Francis Macomber," the action shifts from past to present. This shifting of time is the way we learn what happened and why, and it keeps us interested in the story. But good stories always have all the plot elements in them.

Ask yourself the following questions regarding "A Jury of Her Peers," -- "Why did the author arrange the story elements the way she did? How does she control our emotional response and prepare us for reversals or surprises?"

ELEMENTS OF STORY STRUCTURE

- Inciting Event – the plot device that sets the story in motion.
- Narrative & Exposition – Background information necessary for readers to understand what happens within a story and its protagonist.
- The Real Problem – The dilemma at the heart of the story, inner and outer.
- Internal & External Conflict – Opposing forces that block resolution of the problem.
- Rising Action – The intensification of action, events, and conflicts.
- Foreshadowing, Suspense & Tension – Hints about future events and conflicts.
- Crisis & Climax – The emotional turning point of higher drama and consequences and the highest point of dramatic intensity and/or action where the external plot problem is resolved, one way of the other.
- Falling Action (Denouement: Untying the Knot) – The outcome from the immediate end of the climax, sorting out of what has happened, and finishing small conflicts.
- Understanding & Realization – Often called the "Epiphany." The sudden insight by the protagonist that provides new understanding of events from the past and leads to growth and understanding and fulfillment of a universal need or yearning.

SUSPENSE & TENSION

Suspense Concepts

Suspense might be the most crucial ingredient in your plotting efforts because it quickly arouses reader curiosity.

Keeping this curiosity aroused as long as possible creates those comments like:
"I couldn't put this book down."
"It's an edge of your seat story."
"I was glued to my seat."

With suspenseful storytelling you will immerse the reader so deep into the story they won't let of the book until its very end.

Definition: "Suspense" derives from the Latin word, *suspensus* which means "to hang."

Take your readers to the edge of the cliff and leave them there.

How do you create suspense? By creating a situation where the reader wants something to happen and it isn't happening... not yet.

Or...

Something *is* happening that the reader wishes would stop.

WAYS YOU CAN CREATE SUSPENSEFUL SITUATIONS
* Prospective danger to the character
* Actual immediate danger to the character
* An unwanted confrontation
* A confrontation wanted by one character and not the other
* An old fear that is about to become a reality
* A life crisis that requires immediate action

Now, don't forget to be mean about these situations... Set up a scene that cries for resolution then act irresponsibly and walk away from that scene to deal with other things which will prolong and exacerbate the reader's desperate need for resolution.
* Do NOT eliminate the prospective danger
* Do NOT allow your character to overcome one danger without getting him into even greater danger
* When a character is apprehensive about a confrontation, hold off on the confrontation as long as possible

•   When using old fears that become realities, Do NOT relieve the fear... MAKE IT WORSE than your character could've ever imagined!
•   If a character's life crisis requires immediate action, make the action BACKFIRE, thereby prolonging the crisis

REMEMBER: Your Duty as an Author is to be as mean as you can to your character which, in turn, will make their success that much greater.

You must learn how to frustrate the reader's expectations to achieve suspenseful fiction successfully.

AN EXAMPLE OF SUSPENSEFUL STRUCTURE (remember this is just an example; plus, you'll want to continue this idea throughout your novel, ending in chapter hangs and then skipping away from giving the chapter's the resolution. This plan should follow PURPOSE OF STORY not a rigid structure format.

Chapters / Scene	Scene 1 - Drugstore	Scene 2 - Church	Scene 3 - Railroad Track
Ch. 1 - Beginning Action		Ch. 1 Action + hanging conflict	
Ch. 2 - Skip to Another Scene	Ch. 2 Action + hanging conflict		
Ch. 3 - Skip again to another scene			Ch. 3 Action + hanging conflict
Ch. 4 - Return Action		Ch. 4 Action + hanging conflict	
Ch. 5 - Return Action			Ch. 5 Action + hanging conflict

... And so on, until the end of your book.

Readers long for conflict resolution but it's your duty to avoid resolution at all costs for as long as you can in order to suspend suspense!

REMEMBER: *Action* in storytelling is the equivalent of *Scene* in storytelling.

If you write no action, you don't really have a scene. Scenes with little or no action read more poetically than how fiction should read which requires scene-building, a sense of thrust toward some logical end to the novel. By the way, scene-building should not to be confused with scene-setting. Remember, also, that when you are building your scenes, Do *not* take the reader where he wants to go. Take the reader where *you* want him to go. Taking a reader where he wants to go or where he feels the story is heading can give a trite sense of story, that the story was predictable. This is one of the worst failures of storytelling.

Here is another way to chart out your existing scenes. I use something similar to this to see if I am mixing scenes up enough and also to see if I'm heading in the right direction of where my outline wants me to go, all the way employing suspense building and tension.

	SCENE OUTLINE		
Scene/Chapter	**Location of Scene**	**Characters in Scene**	**Action in Scene**
Scene/Ch. 1	Main Character Sami's home office	Sami alone and her computer	Sami decides to start a rumor about Mariah on Facebook
Scene/Ch. 2	In the grocery store	Sami and Sheryl	Sheryl asks if Sami has heard about Mariah; Sami lies and says "No."
Scene/Ch. 3	At Sheryl's house at one of her "girls'" parties	Sheryl, Betts, Kathy, Sinthia, Babbs	They all talk about Sheryl and how they need to stop allowing her in their group (because of the false info started by the rumor)
Scene/Ch. 4	On the street in town	Mariah, Sami	Mariah sees Sami and asks to meet her for coffee (they have never before been friends so this is a high-tension scene)
Scene/Ch. 5	Sami's home office	Sami only with a brief visit by her husband	Sami is checking the Facebook page for activity. It's nearly gone viral in her town's community. Her husband comes in and she hides what she's doing.
Scene/Ch. 6	Church	Sheryl and Sami	Sheryl asks Sami to come over for her first girls' night— now she's on the inside!
Scene/Ch. 7	Mariah's	Sami and Mariah	After months of putting her off, Sami goes to Mariah's. Mariah is completely undone by now and she asks Sami if she knows about this

			awful rumor. Mariah senses that Sami may have started it!
Scene/Ch. 8	Sami's home	Sami and Beau (her husband)	Sami confesses what she's done. Beau is angered with her and tells her he doesn't know if he can be married to someone who lies because she feels left out.
Scene/Ch. 9	At the beach	Sami and some passersby	She feels extremely guilty and embarrassed and expects everyone who passes by knows what she's done. She believes that Mariah has told her friends who have all but abandoned her.
Scene/Ch. 10	At the mailbox at Sami's home	Sami	She gets a letter from Mariah writing her to apologize to her how complicit she has been in keeping her on the outside and how she now understands how sad she must have been and apologizes for that.
Scene/Ch. 11	At Church	Sami and Sheryl	The climax scene where Sami confronts Sheryl about her excluding her until everything happened with Mariah and that now she's acceptable in her small group. She blurts out that she started the rumor to shine a light on how ugly they have all been—and in the process Sami shines a

			light on her own ugliness.
Scene/Ch. 12	Sami's home	Sami and Beau	Beau tells Sami he needs some time away from her—that she needs to realize her actions, her words have impact on other people's lives
Scene/Ch. 13	Church	Sami and Priest	Sami confesses her sins and the priest gives her some wisdom on how to make things right— with everyone.
Scene/Ch. 14	At the market; at the UPS, at the post office, at the restaurant, at all of the places where people know her and she knows others	Sami and Minnie, the checkout girl (who was always nice to her but who Sami never asked to go for coffee or come to dinner); Sami and all of the other people at different places throughout the community	Sami invites Minnie and about 20 other people she knows in passing over for a BBQ at her house. She refuses to be someone who is keeping people on the "outside" any longer.
Scene/Ch. 15	At the BBQ	Sami and her many friends and Beau	Beau walks back in from being away for 2 weeks when Sami sees him, when he looks around and sees all of the diversity of the people at the BBQ, he knows Sami understands the deeper meaning of her lie—that the rumor led her to a greater understanding that there should never be anyone on the "outside."

The Ideal Architecture of a Suspenseful Novel in Terms of Chapter-building

Chapter 1 – Should end with a turn of events that will leave the reader in suspense because the reader *WANTS* to stay with the characters in this scene and this particular chapter. Try to think, while you're writing, that you will *NOT* give the reader what she wants because we want to suspend suspense and tension. We want to extend the character's trouble until the climax because the reader will relish the trouble and continue reading. The reader wants to see the character win but only after the character has been through hell and back.

Chapter 2 - Now, set the reader in another place with a *different* character. Remember, the reader is still hanging on to what's happened to the character in Chapter 1 and is wanting to find out but understands that she will need to get through this new scene before the author will set her back with the main character and continue where he left off in the first chapter. But we're not letting the reader down just because she's not in the scene with the main character (from Chapter 1). No! What we do now is to end Chapter 2 with a new, even more riveting turn of events that will now leave the reader in suspense for *THIS* chapter as well as the first chapter. So, now the reader now has two chapters she's longing to see resolved.

Chapter 3 – Continue, as with Chapter 2, to set the reader in another new place for Chapter 3 in order to put them into suspense in this new chapter and with the intent to leave them hanging here now. And, as with the previous chapters… *Skip Away Again*! The reader now has three lines of suspense she must see resolved. Now, she's hooked in the story and there is little reason she will set the book down or stop reading.

Chapter 4 – Continue on with each chapter this way until the end.

Think about stories you've enjoyed, stories like the movie CRASH and ATONEMENT by Ian McEwan as well as any other suspenseful stories that continually rise in conflict and to peak until the very point of climax.

Other Things to Remember

- Short chapters seem to move your novel along faster (as do shorter, action-packed sentences)
- Avoid chapters with fewer than three printed pages (they may not engage the reader enough)
- End as if serializing your story—for instance, leaving the story at the end as if the reader will find out more about what's coming "next time," or, "... to be continued"
- Study novels you've read and found difficult to put down
- Study the chapter beginnings and endings in these novels
  - ✓ They usually end with a scene that the author has intentionally left suspended
  - ✓ These same novels usually begin new chapters somewhere else
- Chapter endings should arouse some sense of curiosity in the reader—that sense or longing of wondering what is to come, a sense of trying to figure out what will happen before they actually read what happens, a sense of foreshadowing a situation that will eventually occur somewhere in the novel in order to give the reader some sense of satisfaction that they know exactly what will happen (that's the trick and then to NOT let them know when you ultimately flip the ending with something much more interested than what is expected!)
- NOTE: Be careful about reorganizing your chapters after you've worked to build impact and suspense while writing—you just might reorganize the suspense out of your novel

One more thing I would like to clarify is that *suspense* can be viewed as a <u>structural</u> device. Whereas, *tension* is a <u>craft</u> device and although tension is a technical device, it occurs within the craft, while you're writing.

Tension Concepts

As I mentioned before, our job as writers is to cause trouble, to gossip, to injure people (especially our main character), to hurt people's feelings, to lead people down the wrong path, to basically set our readers up for that great "Aha!" moment. Our job is to do this same thing to all of our characters. We need a real hot mess of injuries of every kind—physical, mental, emotional, and spiritual. Attack the whole person when you attack.

Tension is a palpable physical sensation that we, the reader, feel. Tension is brought on by sudden stress. The onset of stress releases adrenaline, adrenaline makes us shift in our seats, makes our hearts pump, makes our anger switch to flip on and makes us feel excited while we're reading. Reader excitement will always keep readers coming back to your stories.

When our readers' hearts pound, their blood pressure increases, their palms get sweaty and, you know what? Readers want this to happen.

"It is our nature as humans to avoid conflict unless it's not happening to us, then we want to watch, hear & read all about it." ~Sol Stein, STEIN ON WRITING

Tension is felt within seconds or minutes whereas suspense can last over an entire length of a novel.

Have you ever been yelled at by someone you know, sort of, in front of other people who may or may not be related? Your body flushes hot, you get embarrassed, and you are either stumped by the assault, or react instantly and angrily. That's tension.

Tension lasts as long as our characters are in immediate danger or, as in this above example, feel attacked. Tension will occur when our characters disobey.

As human beings our natural instinct is to:
• 	To relieve tension. But as writers fight your instinct because your readers, we crave it!
• 	To find answers to relieve tension. But as writers, our job is opposite--we must create tension not dispel it.

As writers, it is our job to manipulate our readers' emotions.

One Way to create <u>tension</u>:

State a horrid fact that will occur in just minutes (if not seconds)

Examples of stating a horrid occurrence that will happen shortly:

Your character is watching the news and the newscaster says, "A plane is heading straight for the twin towers in NYC."

Your characters are hiding in a dark house that's been bolted shut and whispers, "The zombies are at the door."

Your character is sitting in a packed restaurant with another girlfriend and the girlfriend says, "Here she comes and she heard what you've been saying about her."

Your character is on the ferry and yells out to anyone who can hear her, "A dog just fell into the ocean."

Your characters are in a car that hits ice and is spinning into oncoming traffic and someone cries out, "We're gonna get hit."

When setting up a tense scene, the rule is to use importance first and to set the first, most important point of tension (the highest risk that is directly related to the climax) as close to the beginning of the novel as possible. Joyce Carol Oates says it best this way, "Start with the biggest problem as close to the beginning of the story as possible."

To start this way, with the biggest problem stated, will put the writer in charge of the readers' emotions.

More Ideas for Plotting Situations to Create Tension
- Dangerous work--think about an electrical lineman or trapeze artist
- A bad time approaching (the ticking clock)
- An accidental meeting with someone you don't want to see
- Trapped with someone/thing dangerous (think about The Life of Pi)
- Use of dialogue--calling someone a bitch or stupid

Can you think of any others? If so, write them down.

5 DISTINCT PARTS OF A CRITICAL MOMENT

1. **Name or __PRELUDE__ the set piece** – this part gives the reader a glimmer of your main character's inherent conflict. It fills in information sometimes using subtext, foreshadowing and secondary characters. It's the point when the author uses a hook in the opening scene. It *alludes* to what will come eventually.

2. **__PREPARATION__ the set piece** – this scene precedes the negation scene and the main conflict scene but with subtle touches that contrast the protagonist with the antagonist; and always between the heroine and the hero. In love stories we sometimes view this scene as the first meeting, the first eye contact, the first touch before a first kiss, that accidental bumping into one another. This scene should preview what is going to happen and *directly* foreshadow the set piece.

3. **__NEGATION__ the set piece** – this scene reverses what the reader has been lead to believe. This scene flips a reader's expectations of what is to come and effectively makes the main conflict scene stand out even more.

4. **Write the __MAIN conflict scene__** – should be critical to the flow of the story and should propel the story forward (narrative drive).

Novels often employs three main conflict scenes (or stair steps, see graph) toward the CRITICAL MOMENT where the critical moment *is* the 3rd stair step, the 3rd main conflict scene. Main conflict scenes should be written ending with disaster or surprise, effectively pushing the reader to read more.

Each disaster or surprise will be resolved by the end of the novel.

5. **__CONSEQUENCE__ scene happens immediately after the main conflict scene. The consequence scene provides some sense of realization for the reader (and sometimes for the characters)** – this scene is the most immediate thing that happens after the main conflict scene. It's a "mini-resolution" to this scene. In resolution scenes we can use greater emotions brought out because of this previous main conflict scene. We can reveal partial realizations and truths about the character's inner yearnings and dilemmas. We can justify the conflict scene and its relation to our character's wounds from the past.

Ask yourself, as the author, how does this consequence/resolution scene affect the path of my story? How does it affect each character's decision about the future? What does the conflict scene do to each character's belief system? Does it make the belief system shaky?

With each CRITICAL MOMENT, the preceding group of scenes (the prelude, preparation, negation, main scene & consequence) should be lesser in risk than the next one coming.

If each *main conflict scene* written builds in risk and urgency until you reach the climax, which is the equivalent to the main conflict scene in Critical Moment #3, **then** the middle of your story will not sag.

SAMPLE NOVEL OUTLINE

I. BEGINNING
    a. CONFLICT DEVELOPMENT –
        i. Inciting Event
        ii. Inherent Conflict
        iii. Internal Conflict
    b. CHARACTER DEVELOPMENT
        i. Character – main protagonist
        ii. Character – any others in the protagonist group
        iii. Character – main antagonist
        iv. Character – any others in the antagonist group
    c. SCENE SETTING
        i. Beginning Scenes (place, time, structure, nature, etc.)
        ii. Middle Scenes (place, time, structure, nature, etc.)
        iii. Ending Scenes (place, time, structure, nature, etc.)
    d. THEME/MOOD – for instance: dark/scary; light/funny; serious/instructive; dark/sad; light/sad
    e. METAPHOR – what one word describes your story; for instance, for my novel Drowning, the title was the metaphor
    f. POV Narrator – How will the narrative be written? First person, 2nd person, 3rd person, or omniscient?

II. MIDDLE – RISING CONFLICT
    a. Critical Moment – #1 –
        i. **Prelude** –
        ii. **Preparation** –
        iii. **Negation** –
        iv. **Main critical moment** –
        v. **Consequence** –
    b. Critical Moment #2 –
        i. **Prelude** –
        ii. **Preparation** –
        iii. **Negation** –
        iv. **Main critical moment** –
        v. **Consequence** –
    c. The *Most* Critical Moment #3 (CLIMAX) –
        i. **Prelude** –
        ii. **Preparation** –
        iii. **Negation** –
        iv. **Main critical moment** –
        v. **Consequence** –

III. ENDING
    a. Denouement –
    b. Ending
        i. Resolution
        ii. Epiphany – THE END.

IN THE BEGINNING

In 335BC, Aristotle posited that **all** story-telling takes on a repetitive and specific format. He called this "format" *dramatic structure*.

Simply saying dramatic structure incorporates three things:

A beginning, a middle and an ending.

Sometime in the early 1800s, Gustav Freytag came along agreeing with Socrates' take on dramatic structure but expanding on Aristotle's general theory.

Freytag's analysis became this: FREYTAG'S PYRAMID

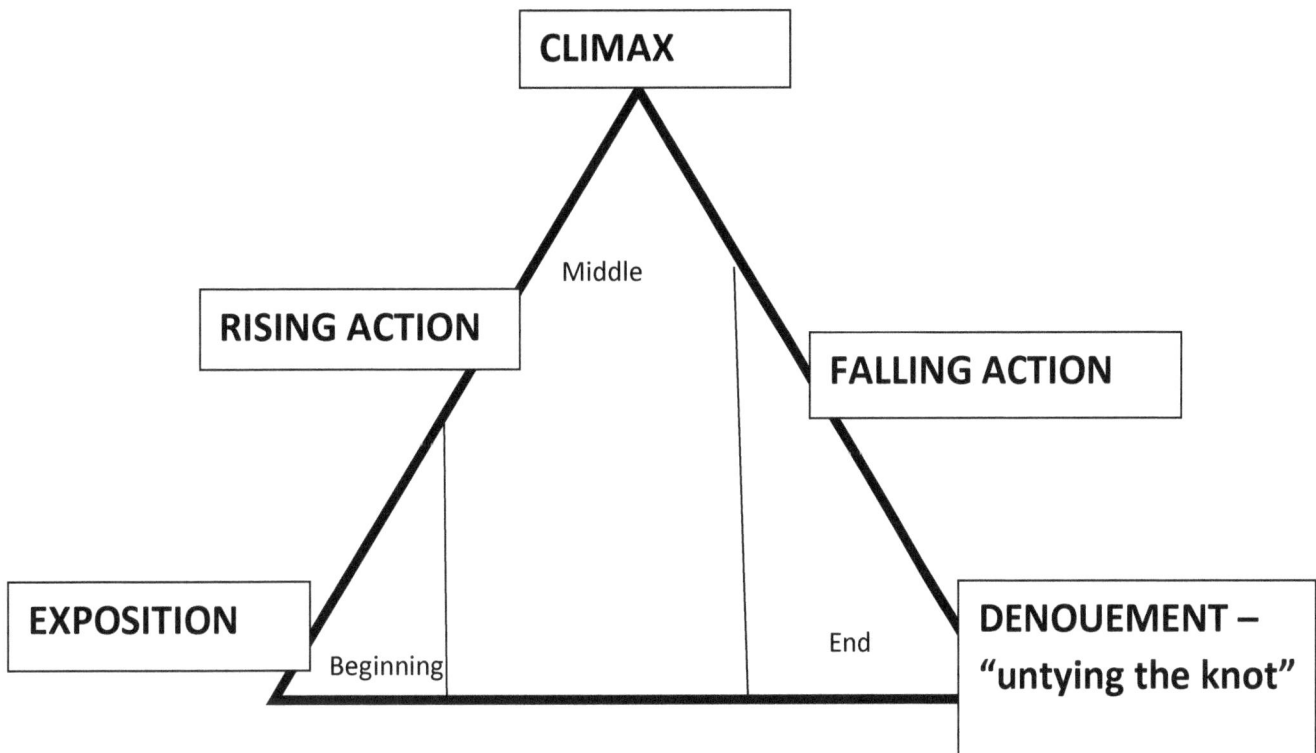

CLIMAX

Middle

RISING ACTION

FALLING ACTION

EXPOSITION

Beginning

End

DENOUEMENT – "untying the knot"

Some 200 Years Later, Here's My Take on Dramatic Structure

Where   is **Bridging Conflict**
That thing that ties the beginning to the
End and threads the story together.

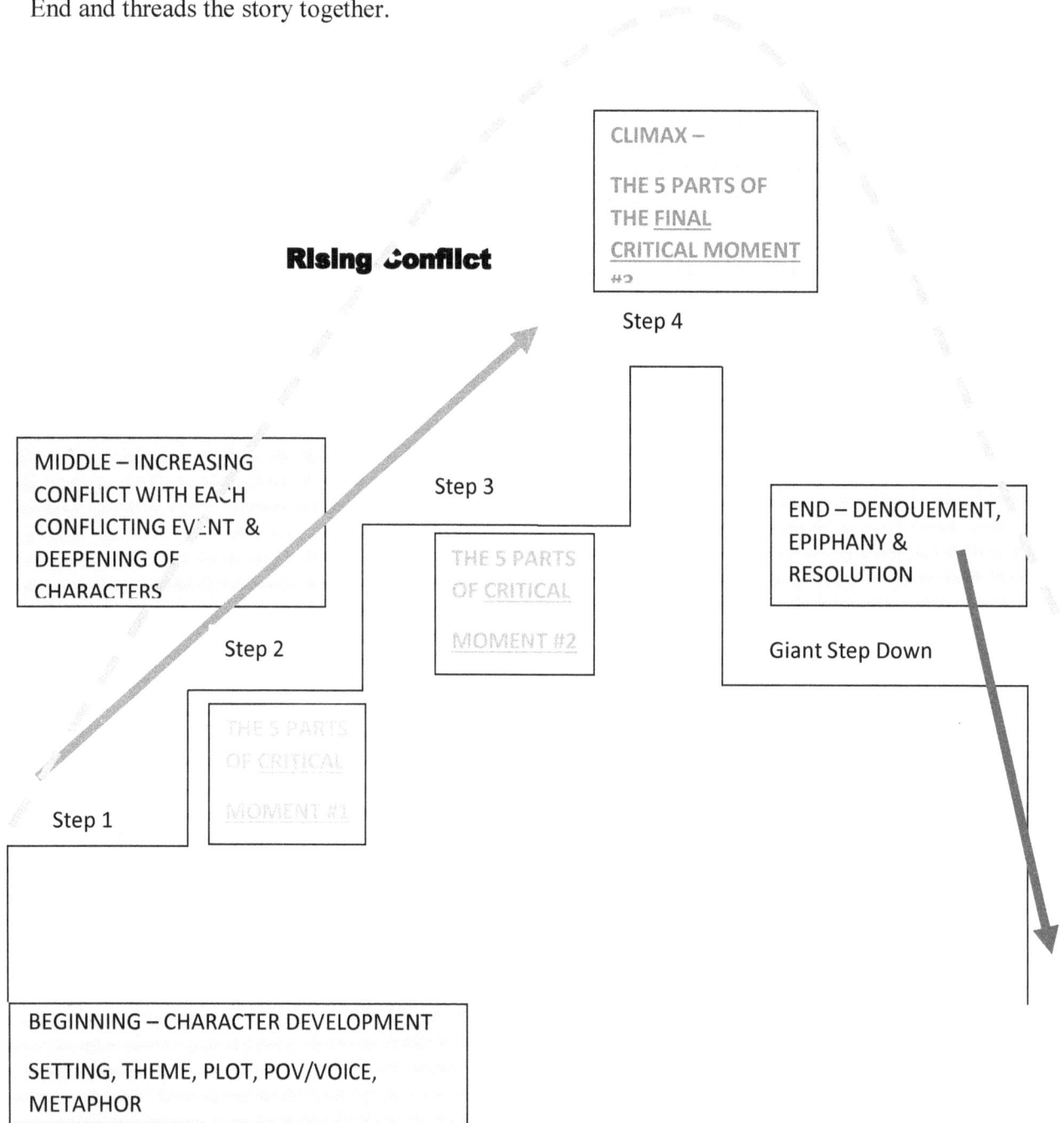

Rising Conflict

CLIMAX –

THE 5 PARTS OF
THE FINAL
CRITICAL MOMENT
#3

Step 4

MIDDLE – INCREASING
CONFLICT WITH EACH
CONFLICTING EVENT &
DEEPENING OF
CHARACTERS

Step 3

THE 5 PARTS
OF CRITICAL
MOMENT #2

END – DENOUEMENT,
EPIPHANY &
RESOLUTION

Step 2

Giant Step Down

THE 5 PARTS
OF CRITICAL
MOMENT #1

Step 1

BEGINNING – CHARACTER DEVELOPMENT

SETTING, THEME, PLOT, POV/VOICE,
METAPHOR

Let's Start at the Beginning

Necessary Beginning Stuff in Writing

Character

Those Developmental, Early Years:

- ✓ When/where was your character born? In the U.S. or abroad? Where in the U.S.? The south or the north? The east coast or the west? In a city or in the country?

- ✓ To whom was she born? What was their heritage? How far removed are the parents from their heritage? First generation or 10th? Is the mother dominant or is the father? Did both parents work or did one stay home? Then, which parent stayed home--the mother or the father?

- ✓ What is the story surrounding her birth? Was it a difficult birth? Was she born on the ferry on the way to the hospital?

- ✓ How did she progress from infancy to toddler (0 to 2 years)? Think in terms of the parents' *and* the character's viewpoint. Was there a sense of happiness about your character's progress? Unhappy? Concerned? Worried for her life? Was she distracted by loud sounds or not? Did she cry a lot? Sleep all the way through the night, or was she up all night long? Was she breastfed or bottle? Did she take to the nipple easily or did she reject it? Did she start speaking before the average, on average, or slower than average? How was her walking? Eyesight? Did she rock in her highchair?

- ✓ How did she progress from toddler (2 to 4 years)? Did she seem removed from children her same age or did she get along well with other kids? If she played with other children, did she share or was she stingy? Was this of her own doing or was her distance from others outside of her control? Was she reading at her level by now or was she far-advanced or slower than average? When she colored with crayons did it seem controlled or messy? Did she point a lot? Was she chatty or reserved? Was she healthy at this age or did she require special medical assistance?

- ✓ How did she progress from 4 to 5 years old? Did she seem happy playing by herself? If not, did the parent distract her with other things, like TV or noisy "educational" or "coordination-building" toys? Did she want to go to preschool or did she hate going to school? What did she notice as routine around her house? Did her parents fight often? Did they smoke? Drink? Did one parent clean too much/too little? Did she have any pets by this age? If so, what--a cat, dog, bird, gerbil, hamster, fish? Did she prefer to stay in her bedroom by herself or out with the family? Did she feel things a lot, rub her hands against curtains and fabrics? Did she prefer rocking chairs to ones that didn't rock?

✓ Overall Years 0 to 5? Were grandparents around much? If so, which ones-- maternal or paternal? Did the maternal & paternal grandparents get along? Did either set unduly spoil your character or did they pretty much follow the rules set out by her parents? Was there a sense of comfort or discomfort when grandparents arrived? Was the environment a quiet one or a loud one and why?

Conflict Building and Three Distinct Type of Conflict

Internal Conflict

Internal conflict deals with personal issues—Think psychological problems, false worries, shame, a past sinful act, anger issues, aging, loss of money or employment, coming required retirement. Internal conflict deals with worries the character has and wishes would go away.

Inherent Conflict (aka the Premise)

Inherent conflict is conflict that sets the story in motion. It may be a lie told, a bomb going off, running from a bad guy, a key character is killed. All of these issues may be placed at the beginning of the story and each sets the story in motion.

External Conflict (aka Plot Points)

External conflict usually begins as the author makes her way in to the middle of the story—the gut of the story. Each external conflict is brought by either another character known as the antagonist or some environmental or social event that prevents the main character from reaching her ultimate goal—to quell her internal conflict and to end the inherent conflict (if at all possible).

Giving Your Characters Depth & Breadth – Expanding Your Character

Do this through: developing a character's meaningful past, the narrative POV, the story's theme, sympathetic characters, by using sensory perception, and dilemma to illicit visualization in the reader.

1. **Meaningful Past** – needs, strengths, and weaknesses: this event should create a significant wound or yearning. This wound (or yearning) should leave the character with:

   a. A need so strong she will be driven to fulfill it,

   b. A weakness (a character flaw) – out of control or possibly beyond the awareness of the character,

c. A weakness that gifts the character with a heroic strength; a strength that makes it possible to reach the plot goal. (i.e., the movie "Conspiracy Theory", Mel Gibson's character or in the book "Lost Souls" by Michael Collins the main male character) – Think of a fault that seems undesirable at the beginning of the story but then changes to be a trait that allows the character to push forward through controversy.

2. **Point of View** – like other tools of technique, point of view is more sophisticated and complex than it appears on the surface; it is the vantage point from which you tell your story; point of view is a writer's power tool for character depth (or lack of depth):

   a. An Objective viewpoint – offers a visual reporting of what is happening in a scene; limits the writer to portray only what is seen.

   b. A Subjective viewpoint – offers a full range of human perception and reaction; as well as nonhuman perception and reaction; allows you to freely use all of the physical sense and to provide inner thoughts and feelings.

   c. 1st Person – most subjective for use by the narrator/main character; uses "I, me, we" pronouns

   d. Omniscient – most objective by the narrator (not necessarily the main character); sometimes referred to as 3rd person omniscient; uses the pronouns "he, she, it, they"

   e. 2nd Person – use by the narrator/main character of the "you" pronoun; very rarely used any longer

   f. 3rd Person Close (sometimes called 3rd person limited) used by the narrator and main character in any given scene; gives the flexibility of 1st person and omniscient points of view

3. **Theme** – use only one statement of theme, one the writer must maintain as true throughout the story; a topic or subject, as of a lecture, sermon, essay; a recurring, unifying subject or idea; and ask yourself, *"why do I (as the writer) care to introduce this theme into my story and will it work?"*

4. **A Sympathetic Character** – is a character with whom the reader will easily relate. Does your character seem to only care about himself or is your character concerned about others, does he worry, call his mother, ask about her sore knee, ask her over for dinner; find out what the vet said about her cat? Think about all the conversations you had today. How did each conversation leave you feeling? Try to incorporate that sense of humanness into your character's thoughts and dialogue. Consider giving your characters a quirk.

5. **Sensory Perceptions** – in this day and age when we can practically smell the food on TV it's incredibly important to include in each scene our sensory abilities of taste, touch, smell, sight, sound, (even extrasensory perceptions). I've heard it told that a writer should include every sensory perception on each page of the book. If you use this as a standard your writing will excel exponentially!

6. **Dilemma (or Conflict) and why is it important to your story?**

   a. <u>Inner Dilemma</u> – should relate to the critical past event of the character (see item #1) and add to the character's personal current conflict and tension. Inner dilemma is the point where the character will ask the question (whether verbally or non-verbally), *"What should I do?"* It's the conundrum period for the character, the fork in the road point in the story, and sets up the critical turning point.

   b. <u>Outer Dilemma</u> – relates to a real external force that blocks your main character's achievement of the goal; whether the character is the protagonist and the antagonist, outer dilemma effects them both.

   c. The most effective type of dilemma is the kind where <u>good battles good</u>.

7. One of the most important aspects of the novel is that each element has **Believability**!

What does a reader remember most about a story? Usually, they remember the characters, and usually the main character. Think about the following stories and who/what you remember about them.

Moby Dick – "Call me Ishmael…"

2001 – "Hello, Dave…"

You might not remember as acutely the type of plotting throughout the story, or even maybe the setting but you remember well-crafted characters.

In Writing Scenes, The Writer Can Accomplish Many Things.

The character can:

1. **Depict a place & time,**

2. **Set mood, and**

3. **Further a sense of theme & metaphor**

Setting scene for place and time should not be simply a laundry list of what is around the place but it should instead show the reader what is there. For instance, take this excerpt from "The Great Stone Face" by Nathaniel Hawthorne.

> ONE AFTERNOON, when the sun was going down, a mother and her little boy sat at the door of their cottage, talking about the Great Stone Face. They had but to lift their eyes, and there it was plainly to be seen, though miles away, with the sunshine brightening all its features.
>
> And what was the Great Stone Face?
>
> Embosomed amongst a family of lofty mountains, there was a valley so spacious that it contained many thousand inhabitants. Some of these good people dwelt in log huts, with the black forest all around them, on the steep and difficult hill-sides. Others had their homes in comfortable farm-houses, and cultivated the rich soil on the gentle slopes or level surfaces of the valley. Others, again, were congregated into populous villages, where some wild, highland rivulet, tumbling down from its birthplace in the upper mountain region, had been caught and tamed by human cunning, and compelled to turn the machinery of cotton factories. The inhabitants of this valley, in short, were numerous, and of many modes of life. But all of them, grown people and children, had a kind of familiarity with the Great Stone Face, although some possessed the gift of distinguishing this grand natural phenomenon more perfectly than many of their neighbors.

Two things about this example, the second sentence adds visual qualities as if we are painting a picture or watching a camera filming a set. It also adds mood and possibly some sense of metaphor.

Here's an example of starting with the main problem as close to the beginning as possible. This example is from one of my latest novels, considered women's fiction/family drama entitled, "The Last Maharajan."

CHAPTER ONE

> *Why would she lie? Why now, knowing she was going to die?*
>
> *Somehow Belle's words felt contrived, forced. Euly Winger had been calling her mother Belle since around the age of fourteen. When Belle showed signs that Euly could treat her as an equal.*
>
> *Her mother's words rung like an indictment, allowing a wisp of a notion making Euly recoil from something that happened long ago, evoking a lingering emotion in Euly, a dreamy memory, caught somewhere between the dead and the living and equally unattainable to conjure.*
>
> *What was it her mother said? The exact phrase, the exact placement of words, the first one and then the next, that stirred in her such a strong reaction?*
>
> *"He's your brother." Was it that simple? No, she had added the word "probably" and, with emphasis.*

First problem: We read that Euly's mother has lied to her.

Second problem: Belle, Euly's mother is dying.

Third problem: that someone Euly knows or has known might be her brother—something Euly obviously hadn't heard before now.

Can you see how setting up the major problem will set the stage for future conflicts?

THE MIDDLE

Writing the middle of your story is simply a continuation of wrapping character and her ongoing sense of internal conflict. However, now—for the middle—you will mix in elements of external conflict. In other words, we will get to see her antithesis, the villain, the evil group, and even a heightened sense of internal conflict growing so that external elements becomes a barrier for our main character's goals or successes. We see other people blocking her way. We get a sense of no matter how our main character tries to reach her goal that something will work to stop her.

Using the outline below, you can see how you will build on risk through rising action. The middle section, if not properly written, can lose the reader's interest. One reason why a reader may lose interest in your story is that you have not employ rising risk techniques properly.

When we begin writing the middle, we want to start with the *least* impactful conflict. What I mean is, you need to start with a stumble at the first instance of external conflict. Seen in the first conflict pitch piece set. By the end, the third and final conflict set piece (also known as the climax) we see the character metaphorically falling off a cliff.

If you have your character falling off the cliff at first, the stumble will have little impact by the end of the book.

Here's an example of rising risk for each set piece:

- The Main Conflict Scene for Pitch Piece Set #1 – Your main character has their car keyed by someone.

Alone, this may just seem like a real pain in the rear. But if you add to the information that your main character is a real estate agent and today, of all days, she is showing a multi-million dollar home to potential buyers who will be riding in her car with her to the home site, a keyed car might make or break the deal.

Then, we step up the risk for the next set of conflict.

- The Main Conflict Scene for Pitch Piece Set #2 – An important message from the potential buyers telling your main character that the buyers need crucial information by end of business that day, goes missing or is not relayed. The buyers finally track down your main character but are extremely disgruntled.

At this point, we can sort of infer that a competitor or jealous colleague has been causing the problems but the character doesn't know this—maybe. You can see how set #1 is less in risk than set #2 where the real possibility of losing a sale is hanging in the mix.

The final conflict scene will be the most impactful thing for risk, danger, and reward and is also called the climax.

- The Main Conflict Scene for Pitch Piece Set #3 (or the Climax) – when your main character shows up way too late to a meeting with the potential buyers, she sees that a colleague has taken over the paperwork and part of the commission will be his as well as your character's. When your character asks "what the hell is going on?" The colleague acts like he was doing you and your clients a favor by "helping out" in your character's absence. Everyone looks around at one another and it all becomes clear that he, the colleague, has been behind the two missed messages and even the car-keying. An argument ensues between the main character and the colleague and the clients see what has happened. The main character looks like a hero once again and gets credit for the full sale of the multi-million dollar home.

But, if we switched around any of these pitch piece sets, the impact of the most risky or dangerous would lose power. Do you see that?

Following this method of writing the middle scenes of any novel will help improve your story and will make your reader continue reading each scene as they amp up in conflict for your character.

THE END

Not really!

Here, for the discussion of the ending, we will look at all its specific parts which are written differently than any other parts in the novel but which take all the other parts in to consideration.

The three main parts of writing the ending scene (or scenes) to the novel include the slowing of action, the denouement, and the epiphany.

The Slowing of Action

The slowing of action is a natural process after any great point of conflict—the car crash ends, the bomb stops exploding, the President gets shot. After each scene there exists a moment of pausing and then regrouping that happens in real life and also with our characters. The slowing of action happens immediately after the climax scene. And, if you review the Middle scene examples for rising conflict, you will see that I infused the slowing of action within the description at the end of the climax:

> (The Pause) Everyone looks around at one another and it all becomes clear that he, the colleague, has been behind the two missed messages and even the car-keying. An argument ensues between the main character, the colleague says something demeaning and cruel and the main character and clients see what how devious the colleague is and what has really happened. The main character looks like a hero once again and gets credit for the full sale of the multi-million dollar home.

The pause not only slows action but it gives the characters and the reader a chance to breathe—to think, "Finally! Our good guy has been vindicated!" It slows the reading process and the scene.

You can see that the denouement is included too. Let's move on to that now.

The Denouement

The word *denouement* is a French word meaning "untying the knot." When we explain points of obscurity, or hidden aspects of trouble for the main character, we untie these knots. We explain how dangerous the antagonist is and the outcome, the sorting out what happened, and finishing small conflicts.

As before, in this same example, I have included the denouement in the description at the end of the climax:

> Everyone looks around at one another and it all becomes clear that he, the colleague, has been behind the two missed messages and even the car-keying. An argument ensues between the main character, the colleague says something demeaning and cruel (Denouement) and the main character and clients see what how devious the colleague is and what has

really happened. The main character looks like a hero once again and gets credit for the full sale of the multi-million dollar home.

You can see in this scene how the conflict is completely finished by the end of the climax scene but in further ending scenes we will learn more of smaller conflicts that have unfolded at the end of the story and wrap them up in the story's ending.

The Epiphany

The epiphany is when someone has a realization of why something has been happening.

The epiphany can happen solely to the main character, the antagonist, the community within the story. The epiphany can also happen to any of these characters in combination or all together. But the epiphany may not happen to any of these characters. The only person who ***must*** understand the story's epiphany is the reader. If the epiphany escapes the reader, the story will fail in its ending.

Here are some examples of genres on when to include different characters in their understanding of the epiphany:

> Most commercial genres of fiction – the main character (always), the antagonist (sometimes or not at all), the community (sometimes or not at all)

> Mainstream fiction, women's fiction – the main character (always), the antagonist (sometimes or not at all), the community (sometimes or not at all)

> Literary fiction – the main character (sometimes or not at all), the antagonist (sometimes or not at all), the community (sometimes or not at all)

As you can see, literary fiction departs from the other types of fiction. In Albert Camus' The Stranger, the main character doesn't get the epiphany—the community does and the reader most certainly does.

POV NARRATOR

Today we will talk about Point of View (POV) Narrator. The three types of POV are first person, second person and third person (*omniscient* and *limited* also known as "close").

First Person POV: Writers use POV for various reasons. Many novels that employ the use of first person feel intimate, almost as if the characters are speaking to you directly or that you are standing there in the scene next to the characters as they act.

Second Person POV: This POV is extremely conversational but difficult to maintain throughout an entire novel. The most famous and successful use of 2nd person POV is in "Bright Lights, Big City" by Jay McInerney.

Third Person POV: The use of this POV is common and sometimes used so that the writer can show action in scenes where the main character might not be present.

Multiple POVs: The use of multiple points of view has seen a rise in recent years and is something that readers are finding they enjoy. There was a lot of discussion in prior years to avoid multiple POVs however, the uprising and the acceptance by readers has pretty much quelled the naysayers.

Genres and POV
- Mysteries often use 1st person narration or 3rd person close (or limited) to be with the detective (the solver of the mystery) throughout the story—this limits the reader's discovery so that the solver of the mystery can enlighten us all near the end of the story;
- Literary fiction uses all POV depending on how much the author wants the reader to see happening before the main character does.
- Thrillers & Horrors will use 3rd person close and omniscient to let the reader see what the main character will be stepping into or coming up against so that we the reader will be thinking, "No! Don't go in that dark room! There's a boogey man in there!"
- Romance novels will often use 3rd person
- Memoirs normally use 1st person.

Voice, in my opinion, is the equivalent of Character. Think about it this way: If we didn't have a body in front of us to know the person we were speaking with and had only phones with which to communicate, then all we have is voice.

The sound of a person's voice is a critical element for creating a believable character—think about the phone for a minute. Now, think about that last phone call you had with a close friend the one where they were upset, happy, angry and tell try to remember how you knew that. How did they phrase their sentences? Were they sarcastic? Were they curt? Were they loud, jubilant or sullen? And how did you know that since you couldn't see them?

You knew because of their voice. What struck you most about the conversation?

Now think about that person's attitude and how everything she said was colored by attitude. Or that she tried to cover her real feelings by trying to sound happy. How did it resonate through her voice?

Think about that right now and write down what you heard and how you knew her mood.

_____

_____

_____

_____

_____

_____

_____

_____

_____

_____

_____

MORE ON CHARACTER "VOICE"

The unique way of speaking is one that only your character has—the way that their speech is only their speech, different from every other speaker of the same language, even with the same job who may have grown up in the same region. How your character's voice is different from everyone else in the world.

After thinking about that, think about what will influence your character's use of language? As well, think about how the following items will influence your character's use of language.

- Their job
- Their socio-economic status and educational background
- Their cultural and ethnic background
- Any other languages they may speak, whether English (I'm assuming most of us are writing in English....) is their first language.
- Who they're talking to in this specific SCENE…and what they're talking ABOUT. There are several different ways we communicate with others.
- Adult-to-adult (how friends and colleagues speak with one another)
- Adult-to-child (how parents speak to their children and other children)
- Child-to-child
- Child-to-adult
- Authority figure-to-subordinate (vice versa)
- How our jobs and jargon dictate our communication with others whether:
    - ✓ Adult to adult, or
    - ✓ Authority figure to subordinate (or vice versa).

Socio-economic status and educational background

Socio-economic status and educational background are vital elements of character, and will influence ways a character will speak. How? Many ways…

- Their educational background and social influences are going to vary widely. Someone who has had the benefit of education, especially "higher" education is going to show that in their grammar, syntax, word choice, and even the subjects they choose to speak about. Someone who is less educated will speak differently, and perhaps be more prone to grammatical "errors" as they show up in common usage, etc.
- Even someone self-educated will be different from the more traditionally educated group.
- What was their field? What did they major in? Is that field their profession now? This will bear on the professional jargon they use, as per our previous newsletter on dialogue. But aside from that, their education or lack thereof will have a direct bearing on their vocabulary.

The Average Vocabulary is Approximately 4,000 Words

They say Shakespeare may have had a vocabulary of 40,000 different words. That's a wide range. Your character will exist somewhere from your average guy to the Bard of Stratford on Avon and everyone else in-between.

Consider where your character's voice fits on this continuum?

But remember, using large or unusual words for a character who is of higher intelligence, try not make him so high-falutin' or that he can communicate better than your reader because he knows such high-falutin' words. Otherwise you risk losing your readers on this alone. But, I hear you ask, maybe he does use high-falutin' words that are obscure. If that is the case, write in what he means when he says these words much the way the writers do on Law & Order who, when they use jargon immediately follow the jargon or larger obscure word with its definition.

This is a rule of thumb: You would do best to stick to those common 4,000 words because if most people communicate with a similar 4,000 words there is probably little that can't be explained by not using them.

Factoid: It is told that Theodor Seuss Geisel (better known as Dr. Seuss) wrote *The Cat in the Hat* in response to a publisher's challenge to use only a specific list of two-hundred words. It was a challenge the publisher didn't expect Seuss to meet. When he did, the publisher challenged him again but this time, the publisher cut the list down to fifty, one-syllable words. Seuss's writing was of *Green Eggs and Ham*—arguably his most famous work.

But just to be clear, I'm not coming out in favor of one-syllable words or multi-syllabic, obscure words. My preference is this: if you know the characters voice implicitly, you will know the words he or she will use.

Use of multi-syllabic obscure words

Think of the guy you know and can't stand. You know who I mean—that over-educated pompous ass that shows up to all of the same parties as you. How does he use his vocabulary and education? To their and other's benefit? Or to lord these obscure over people and to show off?

Use of simple words

Think now about an uneducated person? Are they simply uneducated or are is their IQ below average. Will they be ignorant? Or merely unrefined? Take a look at *Pygmalion* or the story's musical, *My Fair Lady*. Now, think about the contrast between the over-educated priggishness of Henry Higgins versus the "street smarts" or Eliza Doolittle. She doesn't speak with refinement. In fact, she uses a cockney accent which is considered a low-class form of proper English. And is that the entire point of the story. But Eliza is critically intelligent. She has a cogent value system and her own philosophy of life. This is because she isn't put off by the way people sound or look. She has a sympathetic world view, one that Henry Higgins does not. Well, not until the end of the story, anyway. (That, by the way, Higgins' realization by the end of the story is what we call an epiphany)

See now why character development is so critical?

PSST: LET ME TELL YOU THE SECRET TO VOICE IN WRITING

Point of View – like other tools of technique, point of view is more sophisticated and complex than it appears on the surface; it is the vantage point from which you tell your story; point of view is a writer's power tool for character depth.

The Different POVs are:
- ✓ 1st Person –use if "I, me, we" pronouns
- ✓ 3rd Person Omniscient – sometimes referred to as the "God's eye POV"; uses the pronouns "he, she, it, they" – is all-seeing, all-knowing,
- ✓ 2nd Person – use of the "you" "they" pronoun; rarely used
- ✓ 3rd Person – (sometimes called 3rd person close or 3rd person ltd); gives limited flexibility of 1st person and omniscient combined; "she" "he"

Voice – a style we insert as writers into our writing whether authorial voice, character voice or narrative voice. We can do the following with our authorial voice. We can:
- ✓ Write as we sound when we speak as our normal self, or
- ✓ We can take on a different persona.

POV Narrator is the more complex device and what we authors use to tell the story. POV Narrator is the voice the reader hears as they read your story.

Voice

What is "Voice"? How would you describe it? List a few ways you might describe the voice of your character:

_____

_____

_____

What is the difference between authorial voice and character voice?

Well, **<u>authorial voice</u>** is a nuance—that way we, the authors, think and speak and react and bring in to our writing.

Character voice is easiest seen (heard) in our characters' dialogue.

If we decide to use a narrator other than ourselves as the storytelling, the storytelling device becomes an auxiliary character and we will get a sense of that character as he tells the story that he is either intimately aware of details in the story or he is an unreliable narrator. Either way, the reader will get a definite feel for him because using character as the narrator he becomes another character in the story—he's telling the story and is either involved in the story or not.

For instance, the narrator can be someone who has simply heard the story before and is re-telling it. Or, the narrator can simply be the author telling the story (think Ernest Hemingway, Kurt Vonnegut)

The best way to get a sense of distinct storytellers and storytelling voices, read any books from the following authors:

- Zora Neale Hurston
- Raymond Chandler
- James Ellroy
- Truman Capote

YOUR CHARACTER CHART

Full name:_____

Reason or meaning of name:_____

Nickname(s):_____ Reason:_____

PHYSICAL APPEARANCE

Age:_____ How old does s/he look?:_____

Eye Color:_____ Glasses or contact lens:_____

Hair Color:_____ Wears hair how:_____

Weight:_____ Height:_____

Type of body or build:_____

Skin tone:_____ Skin type:_____

Shape of face:_____ Distinguishing marks:_____

Predominant feature(s):_____

_____

Looks like:_____

Is s/he healthy?_____

FAVORITES

Favorite color:_____

Favorite music:_____

Favorite food:_____

Favorite literature:_____

Favorite expressions:_____

_____

_____

Favorite expletives:_____

_____

_____

HABITS

Smokes:_____ What?_____

When and how much?_____

_____

Drinks:_____ What?_____

When and how much?_____

Hobbies:_____
_____
_____

BACKGROUND

Hometown:_____
Type of childhood:_____
_____
_____

First memory:_____
_____
_____
_____

Most important event that still affects character:_____
_____
_____
_____

Why?_____
_____
_____
_____

Education:_____
_____
_____

Religion:_____
Practicing?_____
Why/why not?_____

Financial:_____
_____

FAMILY

Mother:_____
Relationship with her:_____
_____
_____

Father:_____

Relationship with him:_____
_____
_____
Siblings:_____
How many?_____ Birth order: _____
_____
_____
Relationship with each:_____
_____
_____
_____
Children of siblings:_____
_____
_____

ATTITUDE

Most at ease when:_____
_____
_____
Ill at ease when:_____
_____
_____
Priorities:_____
_____
_____
Philosophy:_____
_____
_____
How s/he feels about self:_____
_____
_____
Past failure s/he would be most embarrassed to have people know:_____
_____
_____
_____
If granted one wish, what would it be?_____
_____
_____
_____ why?_____
_____
_____

PERSONALITY

Greatest source of strength in character's personality (whether s/he recognizes it as such or not):_____
_____
_____
_____

Greatest source of weakness in character's personality (whether s/he recognizes it as such or not):_____
_____
_____
_____

Character's soft spot:_____
_____
_____

Is this obvious to others?_____
If not, why not:_____
_____
_____

Biggest vulnerability:_____
Why?_____
_____
_____

TRAITS

Is s/he an optimist or pessimist?_____
_____
_____

Introvert or extrovert?_____
_____
_____

Drives and motivations:_____
_____
_____

Talents:_____
_____
_____

Good characteristics:_____
_____

Character flaws:_____

_____

_____

Mannerisms:_____

_____

_____

_____

Peculiarities:_____

_____

_____

_____

Biggest regret:_____

_____

_____

_____

Minor regrets:_____

_____

_____

Biggest accomplishment:_____

_____

_____

_____

Minor accomplishments:_____

_____

_____

_____

Character's darkest secret:_____

_____

_____

_____

Who, if anyone knows about it?_____

_____

How did this person discover it?_____

_____

_____

PERCEPTION OF SELF

One word CHARACTER would use to describe self:_____ _____

_____

Complete description of how CHARACTER describes self:_____

_____
_____
_____
_____
_____
_____

What does CHARACTER consider best physical characteristic?_____

What does CHARACTER consider worst physical characteristic?_____

Are these realistic assessments? If not, why not?_____
_____
_____
_____

How does CHARACTER think others perceive him/her?_____
_____

What would CHARACTER change about self?_____
_____

Why?_____
_____
_____
_____

If that change occurred, would CHARACTER be as happy as s/he thinks she would? Why or why not?_____
_____
_____
_____
_____
_____

INTERRELATION WITH OTHERS

How does character relate with others?_____
_____

How is s/he perceived by:
Strangers?_____
_____

Friends?_____
_____

Wife/husband/lover?_____
_____

Hero/heroine?_____
_____

CHARACTER'S first impression of hero/heroine:_____
_____
_____

Why?_____
_____
_____
_____

What happens to change his/her perception?_____
_____
_____
_____

What do friends/family like most about character?_____
_____

What do friends/family like least about character?_____
_____
_____

GOALS

Immediate goals:_____
_____
_____

Long range goals:_____
_____
_____

How does s/he plan to see these goals accomplished?_____
_____

_____
_____
_____
_____

PROBLEMS/CRISES

How does s/he react in a crisis?_____
_____
_____

How does s/he face problems?_____
_____
_____

What kind of problems does character usually have?_____
_____
_____
_____

How does character deal with NEW problems?_____
_____
_____
_____

How does character react to change?_____
_____
_____
_____

GENERAL

Favorite clothes:_____
_____

Least favorite clothes:_____
_____

Why?_____
_____
_____

Jewelry:_____

_____

Drives:_____
Why?_____
_____
_____

Place s/he wants to live:_____
Why?_____
_____

Spending habits (frugal, spendthrift, etc.):_____
_____
_____
Why?_____
_____
_____

What does s/he do too much of?_____
_____
_____
Too little of?_____
_____
_____
Most prized possession?_____
_____
Why?_____
_____
_____
_____

UNCATEGORIZED

Who does character secretly admire?_____
_____ Why?_____
_____
_____

Person character is/was most influenced by:_____
_____ Why?_____
_____
_____
_____

Who is the most important person in his/her life before books
starts?_____

Why?_____

_____

_____

_____

How does character spend the week before the book starts?_____

_____

_____

_____

_____

_____

_____

_____

_____

_____

_____

_____

_____

_____

_____

_____

_____

_____

WRITING "THE END" AND NOW THE REAL WORK BEGINS

So, you've just typed THE END on your manuscript and you sit back in your chair and take in a good long breath of air. You say, "I'm done!"

But, wait! There's more.

The best manuscripts, those most likely to get a look at by an agent or publisher, are those in which you go through three separate edits and have finally run the spell-checker/grammar-checker on. That's the first step to really completing your novel. The next step is to hire an independent editor and then a proofreader—both are necessary to show that you are serious about turning over a nearly-perfect manuscript to a professional who can make your career.

Some writers try to do these final steps themselves but no matter how I try, I cannot get completely out of my story to find all of the problems that might exist in my manuscript that I'm just not seeing. An independent eye will see things you, the writer, will not.

I cannot impress enough how important this final step is. Hiring a qualified, independent editor will be one of the best things you can do for your great story. Give it all of the attention you can.

Heck, you've spent months, maybe years writing your story, give it the respect it deserves—the respect you deserve for the time you've committed to the writing.

But, hey, you just wrote THE END. Why don't you sit back and revel in the moment. And, congratulations. You did it.

BLANK PAGES

MY BIG THANK YOU

I want to say thank you to a few people who helped me with this how-to-write workbook...

To my husband, Bob, of course who encouraged me to take my workshop to print and who always cheers me on.

But there are a few more who I would like to list. They are:
Diana Mancel
Mark Woodland
Doug Dutcher
Donna Rich
Melissa Henderson
Sandra Sarr
Mark Sadler
Aliya DalRae
Sue Vancelette Walker
Susan Finlay
Cate Cooper
Erica Miner

Thank you all for taking time out of your busy schedules to help me polish this book into something emerging authors might find useful. I'm indebted to you forever.
~Susan Wingate.

BIBLIOGRAPHY

Over the years teaching how to write the novel, I have drawn from exceptional writing resources and because they have shaped my own success, I feel they must be mentioned. Those exceptional books are:

Sol Stein's, STEIN ON WRITING
Donald Maass's, WRITING THE BREAK-OUT NOVEL
Elizabeth Lyon's, THE WRITER'S GUIDE TO FICTION
Natalie Goldberg's, WRITING DOWN THE BONES
Elizabeth George's, WRITE AWAY
Anne Lamott's, BIRD BY BIRD

I'm sure these are not the only books I've read and drawn from but these books are the ones I return to over and again and the ones that come to mind because they had such a positive influence not only on my own novels but on my workshops for teaching novel-writing.

So, thank you to the wonderful authors of the above list of books.

YOU CAN LEARN MORE ABOUT SUSAN WINGATE

Susan Wingate's Website: www.susanwingate.com

Amazon: www.amazon.com/Susan-Wingate/e/B003CMMERK/

Facebook: www.facebook.com/authorsusanwingate

Twitter: www.twitter.com/susanwingate

If you've enjoyed this workbook, please leave a positive review on the site where you purchased the book. And thank you for reading and using MUSCLE-UP THE GUT OF YOUR STORY: How to Write the Novel by Susan Wingate.

If you are interested in talking with Susan Wingate about becoming a coaching student or want to be included in her next webinar series on MUSCLE-UP THE GUT OF YOUR STORY: How to Write the Novel, please contact Susan at info@susanwingate.com.

www.ingramcontent.com/pod-product-compliance
Lightning Source LLC
Chambersburg PA
CBHW081222020426
42331CB00012B/3070